Go Green
Yourself

The Earth will Thank You

Table

Contents

Go Green Yourself   3

What is Going Green you may ask?   3

Lifestyle.   6

Be Green with Food   12

Green in your home   15

Be Green and Recycle   23

Green Energy   27

Go Green Because...   28

I was a… Farmer earlier in life and I learned a lot of the effects of being Green and its wider effect on the environment and wrote this book as a beginners look at Being Green for the planet.

Enjoy and save the planet. ☺

Go Green Yourself

What is Going Green you may ask?

Going Green is what people across the globe are doing to save and protect the environment. Going Green can be as simple as recycling or as ambitious as building a Green home.

This book will explain the reasons to Go Green along with the many ways that you can use to also go green and be Eco-friendly.

Green = Eco-Friendly, Ok who came up with that little tidbit?

Here are just a few of the examples of how being green has evolved through the years.

The number one and first contribution to the world of recycling is these large creatures of long ago, dinosaurs. That's right the oil we use today in our world started as a dinosaur. So it's only fitting that we say they were first.

Recycling and generally being Green has been around for a very long time.

Did you know that in 1690 The recycled paper manufacturing process was started by Rittenhouse Mill near Philadelphia and can make paper from fiber made from recycled cotton and linens.

In 1874 Curbside recycling like we have today starts in Baltimore, Maryland. In Nottingham, England, a new green device that was called the destructor provided the first systematic incineration of city waste.

1892 The Sierra Club is founded in San Francisco by conservationist John Muir. It is the Americas first environmental organization. Muir was an American naturalist and a well known author and also a very early advocate of the preservation of the wilderness property in the United States.

No one person is the main player in this Going Green movement but there are a few that helped get the word out to the masses.

Henry David Thoreau wrote a book called Maine Woods about saving our forests. That caused a few people to take some notice of our forest. Thoreau was an American author and poet, also a philosopher at times.

In the 19th century George Perkins Marsh also told of the dangers of not protecting what we have before it is lost. Marsh wrote Man and Nature in 1864 and it constituted the very early work of ecology in the 19th century.

The one person most noted in history books for the environment would be Teddy Roosevelt our president that helped make being green a well-known idea. Teddy Roosevelt wanted to protect our wildlife from the dangers of waste and environmental harm. While President Roosevelt put many acres of prime wooded areas under the protection of the forest protection act. The Forest Preserve.

In the seventies the United States passed the clean air act that has done much good for the air that we breathe. In some of our major cities the air quality had become so bad it was life threatening to the old and sick.

The EPA founded in the late sixties to try to regulate the negative impact we were doing to the environment. The Environmental Protection Agency was started on December 2 1970 by President Nixon.

Needless to say green has always been around us in many ways it was just never taken so seriously as it is now. Due to better knowledge of what will happen to our planet if we don't head to warnings of impending ecological disasters the inhabitants of this beautiful planet are beginning to take notice.

This book is a guide for some of the things that you can do every day to Go Green and protect this this Earth the place we call home.

Grab a note pad and write down the things that you can do to become more environmentally sound while you read this book.

Save our planet for the generations to come by Being Green and doing your part today.

You can find more information on how to be green by visiting our website at go-green-yourself.com

Go Green: Lifestyle

You want to be green but don't know where to start?

Lifestyle.

This is the first place for you to start to be green. Your lifestyle dictates just how green you are in your life right now.

By changing just a few things in your everyday lifestyle you can be on your way to doing your part in saving the planet and being Green.

Number one question: what kind of transportation do you use? Do you drive to work or do you use public transportation?

Using public transportation is one thing you can do immediately to lessen your carbon footprint.

Did you know that your car could produce up to 7000 kilograms of CO_2 a year of very un-green gas's every year! Your car can also pollute land and water.

Did you know that the United States uses half of the planets gasoline? ☹

Therefore, you need to invest in the most environmentally safe vehicles that you can afford. Be it electric or hybrid once again the Earth will thank you.

Paper or plastic is something we hear every time we go to the grocery store to buy groceries. Make sure that you always answer paper to stay green.

By just doing this one thing you can make an impact in your local landfill. Plastic bags at your local grocery store started showing up in local stores in the late eighties even though the plastic bag itself has been in use by other stores since the sixties.

Did you know that between five hundred billion and a one trillion **plastic grocery bags** are used in the world each year!

Plastic bags also harm our wildlife. Each year countless amounts of birds and fish die due to plastic bag pollution.

Aerosol products are doing harm to the environment every day. Aerosol products emit chemical particles into our air that have a lasting impact in the quality or the air we breathe.

For most aerosol products there is a non-aerosol equivalent. The next time that you need hair spray or other aerosol product, take the time to find its non-aerosol equivalent.

If we continue to use these products we are at risk of destroying the ozone layer that protects us from the harmful rays of radiation that impact the planet daily.

Try to avoid using aerosol hair sprays, spray paints and air fresheners to name just a few. If the product is dispensed with a gas then its probably not good for the environment.

If you have these products and plan to throw them away remember that you need to recycle them properly to keep them out of your local landfill.

Call your local recycling center to find out more information.

Did you also know that by eating red meat you are also affecting the environment? That's right, buy consuming red meat you are causing gases like methane to escape into the atmosphere. Your red meat comes from cows the makers of methane gas, and lots of it.

Cows supply you with red meat and they also pollute the air that we breathe. The gas is methane and it causes harm every day. I'm not telling you to give up red meat but you can cut your red meat intake down to help be green and cut down on cow farts. ☺

Less red meat consumed means less cows which in turn will mean less methane gas and that alone can make a large impact on our air quality. ☺

You need to become a green shopper. Pay attention to the packaging of a product to see if it uses recycled materials in its packaging. You will read more on this further into the book.

Also look for products that are organic in nature. All of these things can help you go green.

Go Green on vacations. Stay close to home and save gas. Camping is a Green getaway for example. Go sightseeing in your closest large city. Go to museums.

Let's recap what we have learned so far.

1. The Green idea has been around for a long time
2. Petroleum engines have a major impact on the environment.
3. Plastic bags are very harmful to both the environment and wildlife.

4. Aerosol products are destroying our atmosphere.

5. Red meat consumption causes more cows, which means methane gas.

Go Green: Food

Be Green with Food

Go Green by both buying foods that are both organically grown and with Eco friendly packaging.

Why? Pesticides and other chemicals that are being used on food crops have a major impact on the environment.

What are pesticides?

Pesticides are chemical based products used to destroy pest and weeds in most major vegetable farms. Some pesticides are nature in composition and some are man-made.

Man-made pesticides are the dangerous ones for the environment.

These chemicals can leech into our water supply and be hazardous to our health.

Pesticides are applied in the soil or topical to the growth itself.

You can purchase pesticide free foods at most local markets. Look for the organically grown labels to be sure.

If you are a gardener then you can grow your own organic vegetables. By using organic fertilizers and compost you can have your very own organic garden.

Products that use organic or recycled packaging are the ones you should purchase also. The organic packaging is the way some suppliers package their goods in an effort to be Eco friendly.

These companies use recycled materials that are either recyclable or environmentally safe so that the material will break down either in a landfill or the packaging itself can be recycled.

These materials are often made of recycled paper products to products made from plant material. Rice and many other grain fibers have found to be great for making recyclable materials for packaging.

A new breed of plastic bags has now developed using plants as a base material and not petroleum.

Frozen meals in green containers constructed of renewable resources and can also be recycled after use.

The food industry has come a long way into the world of being Eco friendly. It's probably only a few years away from using all green materials in its containers and packaging.

Go Green: Home

Green in your home

Home is a great place to Go Green. There is a huge list of things that you can do at home to make you Green. Let's look at the list.

Paint.

The paint on your walls is a good place to start. Did you know that non Eco friendly paint could release chemicals years after use.

Propylene glycol, Ethylene glycol and Heavy alkanes are just a few of the chemicals that give off fumes.

These fumes are not only harmful to the environment they are also harmful to your health. Many paints are now regulated on the amounts of certain caustic chemicals can be used.

There is a small amount of paints available on the market although they may not be available in your local area. These paints are completely chemical free made from all nature plant materials.

Your house could use a fresh coat of paint anyway. Right?

The lighting that you have in your home can also be Eco friendly. Everyone has seen the new light bulbs that are energy saving available at your local store but did you know that they could also be a danger to the environment?

Mercury used in these new energy saving light bulbs, mercury is ro good for the environment, and it is harmful to you. Yes they do save energy so it is a catch-22.

Did you know that when you turn on that energy saving bulb it emits poisonous materials. These include including phenol, naphthalene and styrene.

Unfortunately these bulbs are the best thing available right now when it comes to saving energy.

The Green alternative is to open your window dressings and let in as much light as possible to eliminate the need for artificial lighting. f you have small windows then now is the time to purchase new energy saving large windows.

Most new energy saving windows will let in the light but not the heat of the sun which in turn will help to save on your energy bill during the summer months.

Skylights also offer a great source of natural light for your living space.

The natural lighting will also show off your freshly painted walls. ☺

Let's talk appliances that save energy. The majority of appliances manufactured today come with an energy saving label telling you the amount of energy the appliance will use on average along with the savings for you on your energy bill.

This program called Energy Star started in 1992 by the EPA to help consumers be more energy efficient.

This program has a set of energy saving guidelines that appliance manufacturers must use in their products. Noncompliance of these rules can have fines that can bankrupt a company.

For example as of 2008, the average refrigerator will need a 20% savings over the normal minimum standard. All appliances have their own set of guidelines.

Tip: Know what you want before you open the refrigerator door and don't leave it opened for more than a few seconds.

Your stove can be either natural gas or electric. Both models are available with tremendous energy savings. Both models are about the same when it comes to being Green.

Tip: Use the oven light to check your food instead of opening the oven door.

Your sink faucet can also be energy saving. The amount of water that comes out of the faucet head may seem the same but the amount of water is actually lower.

New microwaves are to be energy savers. The cooking time has not changed but the amount of electricity needed has lowered.

A bathroom can also be Green. Just like the kitchen faucet they have on the market a large selection of lavatory sink faucets that are energy saving.

When it comes to your shower there are a wide variety of energy saving shower heads. These heads usually have many features such as the pulse among others.

Your hot water for your shower can also be Green by using an on demand water heater. This kind of water heater does not reheat the same water over and over so you will always have hot water it only heats the water when you need it.

This type of water heater is easy to install and has large energy savings.

Lighting in a bath can be energy saving by using energy saving bulbs along with a bright wall treatment and a large mirror to bounce the light to fill them room more.

Skylights in the bathroom have become very popular in new home construction. Skylights that also open are great alternatives to using a bathroom vent fan.

For your heating needs you should have low voltage or water heating built into your bathroom floors.

Finally the throne. Energy Saving toilets are available in all kinds of designs.

These toilets use just a small amount of water that's kept you from flushing your money down the drain. ☺

Electronics in your home can waste energy also.

Even though your big screen TV or your new computer and sound system all came with an Energy Star sticker doesn't mean they are totally Green.

This also applies to your cable box or your satellite receiver, all of these will continue to use electricity even after you turn them off.

When you turn off your electronic devices believe it or not they are still using energy. That's right 99% of these devices continue to draw energy even after you have hit the off button.

One way to fix this problem is to turn off the power bar or a light switch where they are connected.

Turn off your computer when not in use and switch off the surge protector it's connected to. Always remember to turn off lights that are not needed also.

During the summer don't stand at an outside door with it opened to talk to a visitor.

Buy a programmable thermostat to turn your heat or air down to a lower setting when you're asleep or not at home.

Clean your forced air vent system yearly to prevent air flow that can cost you money. Your vent system will become plugged with pet hair, dust bunnies and other materials that will restrict air flow causing energy loss.

Put Plastic on your old windows during the winter to prevent drafts and energy loss. In some situations you may want to leave the plastic on the windows in the summer also to save on your air conditioning cost.

Prevent drafts from around doors with new weather stripping and use a door dog at the bottom to also prevent unwanted air flow.

Install a wood burner and cut your winter fuel bill by half.

Make sure you have the right amount of insulation in your attic to save both winter and summer.

The Government provides an energy saving chart for you to use when calculating the amount of insulation you will need for your particular situation.

Go Green: Recycle

Be Green and Recycle

Go Green with recycling is one of the most popular ways of being Green.

The whole world knows about recycling and many major companies exist just for the business of recycling.

Recycling roots. Recycling has been around for thousands of years in one form or another. People have always found ways to re-purpose things. Recycling really started to take hold on the mainstream population in the seventies.

Recycling centers were set up in local malls for people to deposit materials like paper and glass. Then the beverage distributors started to use aluminum cans and that sparked a new recycling craze. Recycling cans for cash.

In this day and age more and more people are starting to recycle all kinds of precious metals like brass and copper to name a few.

The price of these precious metals makes you think of money every time you see some thrown away.

By recycling you cut down the amount of resources and energy needed to replenish the need of certain products. When you recycle you are being very Green.

How to properly recycle your waste? Follow a few simple steps and Recycle.

Plastics can lay in a landfill for hundreds or even thousands of years. You should take special care to recycle all of your plastics. Contact your refuse hauler and see if they provide a recycling program that you can use.

If your refuse hauler has no available recycling program then get in touch with your local recycling centers and get any rules you may need to follow for recycling your plastics.

Metals as I said earlier are becoming the new craze for re-cycler because now they get paid money to Go Green and recycle at the same time.

Paints and lubricants have to be recycled properly to prevent the chance of the chemicals reaching your water supply and also contaminating the soil.

Contact your local city government or recycling center for more information.

Aerosol cans have special needs also when it comes to recycling. The leftover propellants and gases in these cans need to be recovered or disposed of in a very special manner so to keep the threat of them being released into the atmosphere.

Garden chemicals and fertilizers also must be recycled in a proper way so that they cannot harm the environment. Do not flush garden chemicals down your toilet or down a sewer pipe, as it will eventually find its way into your drinking water.

Recycling is achievable with countless other things to save energy and be Eco friendly.

Donate your clothes to a goodwill store to Be Green or donate your old eyeglasses to the Lions club. If you're buying a new computer then donate your old one to a local student that can't afford to buy one.

When you recycle products like these you are saving energy in the long run.

Do you need a new hearing aid? You can recycle an old working hearing aid just as if you recycled your old eyeglasses.

Printer out of ink? Recycle your empty ink cartridges to Be Green and save yourself money.

A new set of tires on your vehicle? Recycle your old tires for playground material.

You can see now that when it comes to recycling you have a lot of different ways for you to Be Green. Whether you go full force into recycling or you just try to do your best, you have still been Green and making an impact on the Environment.

Go Green: Energy Sources

Green Energy

Go Green by using Eco friendly Energy using a renewable resource for your home and business electrical needs?

Today's technologies offer offers us a few ways that as home owners or small business can now use Green Energy instead of nonrenewable energy.

Wind Turbines. Windmills and wind collectors have been around for centuries. Now with all of the new technology we are able to harness the kinetic energy and turn it into a Green Energy source.

Solar Energy. Collectors made of a special gathering material turn the suns rays into renewable energy in millions of locations across the planet. These panels and accessories are widely available to the public as DIY kits.

New home construction using solar panels has jumped in the past few years as more homeowners realize the massive savings on their energy bills along with the knowledge they are doing good for the environment.

Why Go Green?

Go Green Because...

Go Green because if we don't do something our lack of being green will destroy the planet Earth. That's a proven fact that needs to be addressed right now in our time before its too late. Your great grandchildren will never know what it's like to walk in the forest. They will never be able to drink from a stream and so on.

You must choose wisely your use of the environment to assure that these little pleasures among many are here for centuries to come for the inhabitants of this planet to enjoy.

Go Green

The Earth will Thank You.